Murat Durmus

Taxonomy of the

most commonly used

Machine Learning Algorithms

Copyright © 2022 Murat Durmus

ISBN: 9798442041989

Cover design:

Murat Durmus

About the Author

Murat Durmus is CEO and founder of AISOMA (a Frankfurt am Main (Germany) based company specialized in AI-based technology development and consulting) and Author of the books "THE AI THOUGHT BOOK".& INSIDE ALAN TURING"

You can get in touch with the author via:

- LinkedIn: https://www.linkedin.com/in/ceosaisoma/
- E-Mail: murat.durmus@aisoma.de

"All models are wrong,

but some are useful."

George E. P. Box

Contents

Introduction

Machine learning refers to the development of AI systems that can perform tasks due to a "learning process" based on data. This is in contrast to approaches and methods in symbolic AI and traditional software development, which are based on embedding explicit rules and logical statements in the code. ML is at the heart of recent advances in statistical AI and the methodology behind technological achievements such as computer programs that outperform humans in tasks ranging from medical diagnosis to complex games. The recent surge of interest in AI is largely due to the achievements made possible by ML. As the term "statistical AI" suggests, ML draws on statistics and probability theory concepts. Many forms of ML go beyond traditional statistical methods, which is why we often think of ML as an exciting new field. However, despite the hype surrounding this technological development, the line between ML and statistics is blurred. There are contexts in which ML is best viewed as a continuum with traditional statistical methods rather than a clearly defined separate field. Regardless of the definitional boundaries, ML is often used for the same analytical tasks that conventional statistical methods have been used for in the past. ML Approaches

ML is a very active area of research that encompasses a broad and ever-evolving range of methods. Three primary approaches can be distinguished at a high level: **supervised learning**, **unsupervised learning**, and r**einforcement learning**.

3

Supervised Learning

In supervised learning, the task of the ML algorithm is to infer the value of a predefined target variable (or output variable) based on known values of feature variables (or input variables). The presence of labeled data (i.e., data with known values for the target in question) is a prerequisite for supervised learning. The learning process consists of developing a model of the relationship between feature and target variables based on labeled training data. This process is also referred to as "model training." After a successful training phase (which is confirmed by a testing phase also based on labeled data), the resulting model can be applied to unlabeled data to infer the most likely value of the target variable. This is referred to as the inference phase.

Supervised learning can solve two main types of analytic problems:

- **Regression problems** where the target variable of interest is continuous. Examples include predicting future stock prices or insurance costs.
- **Classification problems**, where the target of interest is a categorical variable. These include issues where the target variable is binary (e.g., whether a financial transaction is fraudulent or non-fraudulent) and multi-class problems that involve more than two categories. For example, classification can be used to assess the likelihood that customers will default on loan repayments.

4

Unsupervised Learning

Unsupervised learning involves identifying patterns and relationships in data without a predefined relationship of interest. Unlike supervised learning, this approach does not rely on labeled training data. Therefore, unsupervised learning can be more exploratory, although the results are not necessarily less meaningful.

Unsupervised learning is beneficial when labeled data is unavailable or expensive to produce. This approach can be used to solve problems such as the following:

Cluster analysis involves grouping units of observations based on similarities and dissimilarities between them. Examples of tasks where cluster analysis can be helpful include customer segmentation exercises.

Association analysis, where the goal is to identify salient relationships among variables within a data set. Association rules (i.e., formal if-then statements) typically describe such relationships. These rules can lead to findings such as "customers interested in X are also interested in Y and Z." Association analysis is used for product recommendation and customer service management tasks.

Reinforcement Learning

Reinforcement learning is based on the concept of an "agent" exploring an environment. The agent's task is to determine an optimal action or sequence of steps (the goal of interest) in response to its environment. The learning process does not rely on examples of "correct responses." Instead, it depends on a reward function that provides feedback on the actions taken. The agent strives to maximize its reward and thus improve its performance through an iterative process of trial and error.

Reinforcement learning is practical when the optimal actions (i.e., the correct responses) are unknown. In such situations, labeled training data are not available or risk producing suboptimal results when analysts use supervised learning. The conceptual structure of the approach also makes it relevant for problem types that have a sequential or dynamic nature. Examples include problems in robotics or games.

Much work on reinforcement learning is taking place in the context of basic research. This includes research in general AI. Compared to other ML approaches, reinforcement learning is less common in business. The most noted business applications are outside of financial services and include autonomous vehicles and other forms of robotics. Potential applications in financial services include trading or trade execution and dynamic pricing.

These three approaches include a variety of ML methods such as linear regression, decision trees, support vector machines, artificial neural networks, and ensemble methods. However, two general points about methodological differences are worth noting.

First, ML methods differ significantly in complexity. Discussions of ML often focus on practices with a high degree of complexity. For example, neural networks, a family of techniques that search for patterns and relationships in data sets using network structures similar to those found in the biological brain, receive considerable attention. However, ML also includes fewer complex methods such as ordinary least squares regression and logistic regression. These more straightforward methods have long been used in statistics and econometrics and were established before ML emerged in its current form. We will return to the issue of complexity and its practical implications in later chapters. It should be noted that ML as a field encompasses specific, highly complex methods but is not limited to them.

Second, ML methods can be used to design static or dynamic systems. For static systems, ML is used to develop models that do not evolve once they are deployed unless a new model intentionally replaces them. In dynamic systems, on the other hand, models continue to adapt after deployment based on new data that becomes available during operation.

Such dynamic (or incremental) learning can greatly benefit situations where the data available during development is limited or where models capture phenomena with rapidly changing characteristics.

The Taxonomy used in this book

Main Domain and Data Types

Main Domain	Data Type	Definition
Computer Vision	Image	Visual representation of a pixel matrix consisting of one channel for black and white images, three elements for color images (RGB), or four elements for color images with opacity (RGBA).
	Video	A succession of images (frames), sometimes grouped with a time series (a sound).
NLP / Speech Processing	Text	A succession of characters (e.g., a tweet, a text field).
	Time Series	A series of data points (e.g., numerical) indexed in time order.
Classic Data Science	Structured Data	Data is organized in a predefined array model with a specific column for each characteristic (e.g., text, numeric data, date). To be more precise, structured data refers to organized data found, for example, in a relational database (which, as mentioned, may contain columns of text). Quantitative data can be distinguished from qualitative data. Quantitative data correspond to numeric data that can support some arithmetic operations, while qualitative data are usually used as categorical data to classify data according to their similarities.

Learning paradigms with subtypes.

Learning Paradigm	Subtype	Definition
Supervised Learning	Classification	Classification is the process of predicting the class of given data points. (Is the picture a cat or a dog?)
	Regression	Regression models are used to predict a continuous value. (Predict the price of a house based on its features).
Unsupervised Learning	Clustering	Clustering is the task of dividing data points into multiple groups so that data points in the same groups are more similar to each other than the data points in the other groups.
	Dimensionality Reduction	Dimensionality reduction refers to techniques for reducing the number of input variables in the training data.
Reinforcement Learning	Rewarding	The reward is an area of ML that deals with how intelligent agents should act in an environment to maximize the notion of cumulative reward by learning from their experiences through feedback.

Explainability

An important aspect of AI security is explainability. Understanding the algorithms and making them explainable makes them accessible to as many people as possible. In addition, explainability helps increase the trustworthiness of AI and supports forensics and analysis of decisions.

ADABOOST

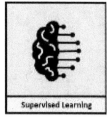 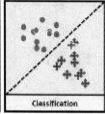 

| Supervised Learning | Classification | Regression | EXPLAINABLE |

Definition	**AdaBoost uses multiple iterations to create a single composite strong learner by iteratively adding weak learners. In each training phase, a new weak learner is added to the ensemble and a weight vector is adjusted to focus on examples that were misclassified in previous rounds.**	
Main Domain	**Classic Data Science**	
Data Type	**Structured Data**	
Data Environment	**Supervised Learning**	
Learning Paradigm	**Classification, Regression**	
Explainability	**Explainable**	

ADAM OPTIMIZATION

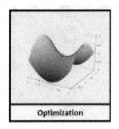

Optimization

Definition	**Adam optimization is an extension of stochastic gradient descent. It can be used instead of classical stochastic gradient descent to update the network weights more efficiently thanks to two methods: adaptive learning rate and momentum.**
Main Domain	**Classic Data Science**
Data Type	**Structured Data**
Data Environment	-
Learning Paradigm	**Optimization**
Explainability	-

AGGLOMERATIVE CLUSTERING

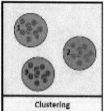

Definition	**Agglomerative clustering is a "bottom-up" approach to hierarchical clustering. Each observation starts in its cluster, and cluster pairs are merged as they move up the hierarchy.**
Main Domain	**Classic Data Science**
Data Type	**Structured Data**
Data Environment	**Unsupervised Learning**
Learning Paradigm	**Clustering**
Explainability	**-**

ARMA/ARIMA MODEL

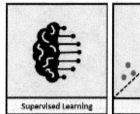
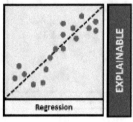

Definition	Given a time series Xt, the ARMA/ARIMA model is a tool for understanding and predicting the future values of this series. The model consists of an autoregressive part (AR) and a moving average part (MA).
Main Domain	Classic Data Science
Data Type	Time Series
Data Environment	Supervised Learning
Learning Paradigm	Regression
Explainability	Explainable

BERT

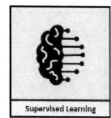 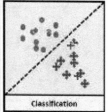

Definition	**Bidirectional Encoder Representations from Transformers (BERT) is a Transformer-based ML technique for natural language processing (NLP) pre-training developed by Google.**
Main Domain	**NLP & Speech Processing**
Data Type	**Text**
Data Environment	**Supervised Learning**
Learning Paradigm	**Classification**
Explainability	**Not Explainable**

CONVOLUTIONAL NEURAL NETWORK

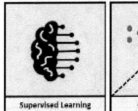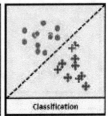

Supervised Learning	Classification

Definition	**A convolutional neural network is a deep learning algorithm that takes an input, assigns meaning (learnable weights and biases) to different aspects/objects in the data, and can distinguish between them.**
Main Domain	**Computer Vision, NLP & Speech processing**
Data Type	**Image, video, text, time series**
Data Environment	**Supervised Learning**
Learning Paradigm	**Classification**
Explainability	**Not Explainable**

DBSCAN

 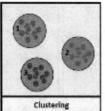

Definition	**DBSCAN - Density-Based Spatial Clustering of Applications with Noise is a density-based, nonparametric clustering algorithm: given a set of points in a shared space, points that are close together (points with many near neighbors) are grouped and points that are alone in low-density regions (whose nearest neighbors are too far away) are marked as outliers.**
Main Domain	**Computer Vision**
Data Type	**Image**
Data Environment	**Unsupervised Learning**
Learning Paradigm	**Clustering**
Explainability	-

DECISION TREE

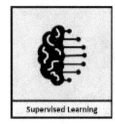 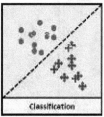 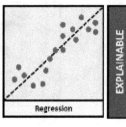

Definition	A decision tree is a diagram that uses a branching method to illustrate every possible output for a given input to decompose complex problems.
Main Domain	Classic Data Science
Data Type	Structured Data
Data Environment	Supervised Learning
Learning Paradigm	Classification, Regression
Explainability	Explainable

DEEP Q-LEARNING

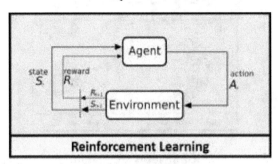

Reinforcement Learning

Definition	**Deep Q-learning works as a Q-learning algorithm because it uses a neural network to approximate the Q-value function to manage many states and actions.**
Main Domain	**Classic Data Science**
Data Type	**Time Series**
Data Environment	**Reinforcement Learning**
Learning Paradigm	**Rewarding**
Explainability	**-**

EFFICIENTNET

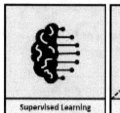 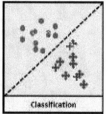

Supervised Learning	Classification

Definition	**EfficientNet is a Convolutional Neural Network based on depth-wise convolutions, making it lighter than other CNNs. It also allows scaling the model with a unique lever: the compound coefficient.**
Main Domain	**Classic Data Science**
Data Type	**Image**
Data Environment	**Supervised Learning**
Learning Paradigm	**Classification**
Explainability	**Not Explainable**

FACTOR ANALYSIS OF CORRESPONDENCES

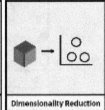

Definition	The factorial correspondence analysis (CFA) is a statistical method of data analysis that allows the analysis and prioritization of the information contained in a rectangular table of data and which is mainly used to study the link between two variables (qualitative or categorical).
Main Domain	**Classic Data Science**
Data Type	**Structured Data**
Data Environment	**Unsupervised Learning**
Learning Paradigm	**Dimension Reduction**
Explainability	

GAN

Definition	A GAN is a generative model where two networks are placed in the competition. The first model is the generator; it generates a sample (e.g., an image), while its opponent, the discriminator, tries to detect whether a sample is real or the result of the generator. Both improve on the performance of the other.
Main Domain	**Computer Vision**
Data Type	**Image, Video**
Data Environment	**Unsupervised Learning**
Learning Paradigm	-
Explainability	-

GMM

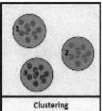

Unsupervised Learning	Clustering

Definition	A Gaussian mixture model is a probabilistic model that assumes that all data points are generated from a mixture of a finite number of Gaussian distributions with unknown parameters.
Main Domain	Computer Vision, NLP & Speech Processing
Data Type	Text, Time Series, Image, Video,
Data Environment	Unsupervised Learning
Learning Paradigm	Clustering
Explainability	-

GPT-3

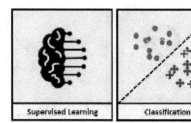

Definition	**Generative Pre-trained Transformer 3 (GPT-3) is an autoregressive language model that uses Deep Learning to generate human-like text.**
Main Domain	**NLP & Speech Processing**
Data Type	**Text**
Data Environment	**Supervised Learning**
Learning Paradigm	**Classification**
Explainability	**Not Explainable**

GRADIENT BOOSTING MACHINE

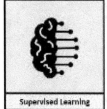 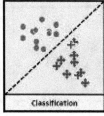 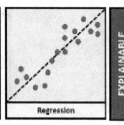

Supervised Learning	Classification
Regression	EXPLAINABLE

Definition	**Gradient boosting is a technique that optimizes a decision tree by combining weak models to improve model prediction.**
Main Domain	**Classic Data Science**
Data Type	**Structured Data**
Data Environment	**Supervised Learning**
Learning Paradigm	**Classification, Regression**
Explainability	**Explainable**

GRADIENT DESCENT

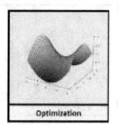

Optimization

Definition	**Gradient descent is a first-order iterative optimization algorithm for finding a local minimum of a differentiable function. The idea is to take repeated steps in the opposite direction of the function's gradient (or approximate gradient) at the current point because this is the direction of steepest descent.**
Main Domain	**Classic Data Science**
Data Type	**Structured Data**
Data Environment	-
Learning Paradigm	**Optimization**
Explainability	-

GRAPH NEURAL NETWORKS

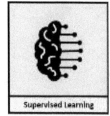  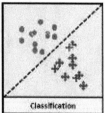

Definition	Graph neural networks (GNNs) are deep learning-based methods that operate on graph domains. Graphs are a kind of data structure that models a set of objects (nodes) and their relationships (edges)
Main Domain	Computer Vision, Speech Processing
Data Type	Image
Data Environment	Supervised Learning
Learning Paradigm	Regression, Classification
Explainability	-

HIERARCHICAL CLUSTERING

Definition	**Hierarchical clustering is a cluster analysis method that seeks to build a hierarchy of clusters. The result is a tree-based representation of the objects, named a dendrogram.**
Main Domain	**Classic Data Science**
Data Type	**Structured Data**
Data Environment	**Unsupervised Learning**
Learning Paradigm	**Clustering**
Explainability	-

HIDDEN MARKOV MODEL (HMM)

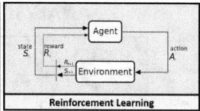

Definition	**Hidden Markov Model is a statistical Markov model in which the modeled system is assumed to be a Markov process with unobservable hidden states.**
Main Domain	**Structured Data, NLP & Speech Processing**
Data Type	**Reinforcement Learning**
Data Environment	**Unsupervised Learning**
Learning Paradigm	**Rewarding**
Explainability	**-**

INDEPENDENT COMPONENT ANALYSIS

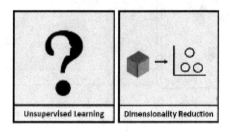

Definition	ICA is a particular case of blind source separation. A typical example application is the "cocktail party problem" of listening in on one person's speech in a noisy room.
Main Domain	Classic Data Science
Data Type	Structured Data
Data Environment	Unsupervised Learning
Learning Paradigm	Dimension Reduction
Explainability	-

ISOLATION FOREST

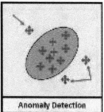

Definition	The isolation forest returns the anomaly score of each sample. It isolates observations by randomly selecting a feature and then randomly selecting a split value between the maximum and minimum values of the selected feature.
Main Domain	**Classic Data Science**
Data Type	**Structured Data**
Data Environment	**Unsupervised Learning**
Learning Paradigm	**Anomaly Detection**
Explainability	-

K-MEANS

 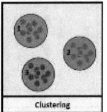

Definition	**K-means clustering is a method of vector quantification that aims to partition n observations into k clusters. Each observation belongs to the cluster with the nearest mean (cluster centers or cluster centroid), serving as a cluster prototype.**
Main Domain	**Classic Data Science**
Data Type	**Structured Data**
Data Environment	**Unsupervised Learning**
Learning Paradigm	**Clustering**
Explainability	**-**

K-NEAREST NEIGHBOUR

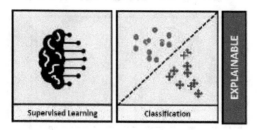

Definition	K-Nearest Neighbor is a simple algorithm that stores all available cases and classifies the new data or cases based on a similarity measure. It is mostly used to classify a data point based on the classification of its neighbors.
Main Domain	Classic Data Science
Data Type	Structured Data
Data Environment	Supervised Learning
Learning Paradigm	Classification
Explainability	Explainable

LINEAR REGRESSION

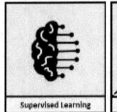
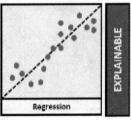

Definition	**Linear regression attempts to model the relationship between two or more variables by fitting a linear equation to the observed data. One variable is considered the explanatory variable, and the other is regarded as the dependent variable. For example, a modeler might want to use a linear regression model to relate the weights of individuals to their height.**
Main Domain	**Classic Data Science**
Data Type	**Structured Data**
Data Environment	**Supervised Learning**
Learning Paradigm	**Regression**
Explainability	**Explainable**

LOGISTIC REGRESSION

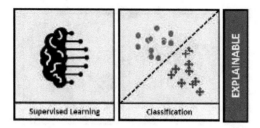

Definition	Logistic regression is used to classify data by modeling the probability of having a particular class or event, such as pass/fail, won/lost, alive/dead, or healthy/sick. This can be extended to model multiple classes of events, e.g., to determine if an image contains a cat, dog, tiger, etc.
Main Domain	**Classic Data Science**
Data Type	**Structured Data**
Data Environment	**Supervised Learning**
Learning Paradigm	**Classification**
Explainability	**Explainable**

LSTM

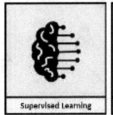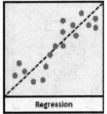

Definition	**Long short-term memory (LSTM) is an artificial recurrent neural network (RNN) architecture used in deep learning. Unlike standard feedforward neural networks, the LSTM has feedback connections. As a result, it can process individual data points (e.g., images) and entire data sequences (e.g., speech or video).**
Main Domain	**NLP & Speech Processing, Computer Vision**
Data Type	**Text, Image, Video**
Data Environment	**Supervised Learning**
Learning Paradigm	**Regression**
Explainability	**Not Explainable**

MEAN SHIFT

 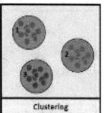

Definition	Mean shifting is a nonparametric feature space analysis procedure for finding the maxima of a density function, a so-called mode seeking algorithm.
Main Domain	**Computer Vision**
Data Type	**Image, Video**
Data Environment	**Unsupervised Learning**
Learning Paradigm	**Clustering**
Explainability	-

MOBILENET

Definition	**MobileNets are based on a streamlined architecture that uses depth-wise separable convolutions instead of convolutions to build light wFeight deep neural networks.**
Main Domain	**Computer Vision, Classic Data Science, NLP & Speech Processing**
Data Type	**Image, Video, Text, Time Series, Structured Data**
Data Environment	**Unsupervised Learning**
Learning Paradigm	**Clustering**
Explainability	**-**

MONTE CARLO ALGORITHM

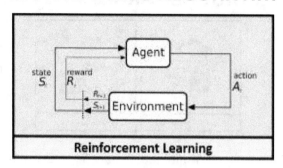

Reinforcement Learning

Definition	A Monte Carlo algorithm is a randomized algorithm whose output may be incorrect with a particular (typically small) probability.
Main Domain	**Classic Data Science**
Data Type	**Structured Data**
Data Environment	**Reinforcement learning**
Learning Paradigm	**Rewarding**
Explainability	-

MULTIMODAL PARALLEL NETWORK

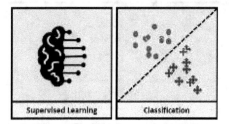

Definition	A Multimodal Parallel Network helps to manage audio-visual event localization by processing both audio and visual signals simultaneously.
Main Domain	Computer Vision, Speech Processing
Data Type	Video
Data Environment	Supervised Learning
Learning Paradigm	Classification
Explainability	-

NAIVE BAYES CLASSIFIERS

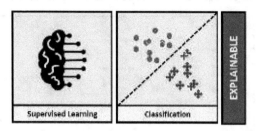

Definition	**Naive Bayes classifiers are a family of simple probabilistic classifiers based on applying the Bayes theorem with strong (naive) independence assumptions between features.**
Main Domain	**Classic Data Science**
Data Type	**Structured Data**
Data Environment	**Supervised Learning**
Learning Paradigm	**Classification**
Explainability	**Explainable**

PROXIMAL POLICY OPTIMIZATION

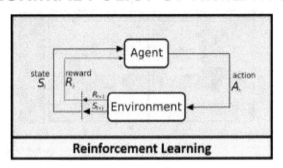

Reinforcement Learning

Definition	**A family of policy gradient methods for Reinforcement Learning that alternate between sampling data and optimizing a surrogate objective function using stochastic gradient ascent.**
Main Domain	**Classic Data Science**
Data Type	**Structured Data, Time Series**
Data Environment	**Reinforcement Learning**
Learning Paradigm	**Rewarding**
Explainability	**-**

PRINCIPAL COMPONENT ANALYSIS

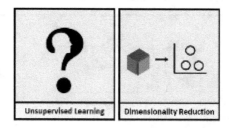

Unsupervised Learning	Dimensionality Reduction

Definition — **The basic idea of principal component analysis (PCA) is to reduce the dimensionality of a data set consisting of many variables that are either strongly or slightly correlated with each other while preserving as much as possible the variation present in the data set.**

Main Domain — **Classic Data Science**

Data Type — **Structured Data**

Data Environment — **Unsupervised Learning**

Learning Paradigm — **Dimension Reduction**

Explainability — -

Q-LEARNING

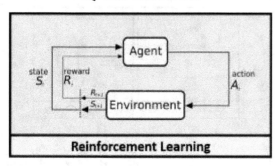

Definition	Q-learning is a model-free reinforcement learning algorithm for learning the value of an action in a given state. It does not require a model of the environment.
Main Domain	Classic Data Science
Data Type	Structured Data, Time Series
Data Environment	Reinforcement Learning
Learning Paradigm	Rewarding
Explainability	-

RANDOM FORESTS

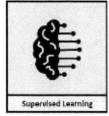
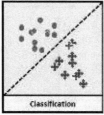
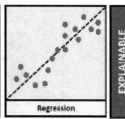

Definition	Random forests are an ensemble learning method that operates by constructing many decision trees at training time and outputting the class that is the mode of the classes (classification) or mean/average prediction (regression) of the individual trees.
Main Domain	Classic Data Science
Data Type	Structured Data
Data Environment	Supervised Learning
Learning Paradigm	Classification, Regression
Explainability	Explainable

RECURRENT NEURAL NETWORK

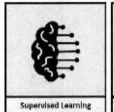
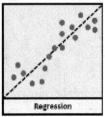

Supervised Learning | Regression

Definition	A recurrent neural network (RNN) is a class of artificial neural networks where connections between nodes form a directed graph along a temporal sequence. This allows it to exhibit material dynamic behavior. Computer Vision, NLP & Speech processing
Main Domain	Computer Vision, NLP & Speech Processing
Data Type	Time series, Text, Image, Video
Data Environment	Supervised Learning
Learning Paradigm	Regression
Explainability	Not Explainable

RESNET

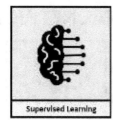 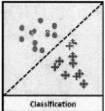

Supervised Learning | Classification

Definition	**A residual neural network (ResNet) is an artificial neural network (ANN) that builds on constructs known from pyramidal cells in the cerebral cortex by using jump connections or shortcuts to skip some layers.**
Main Domain	**Computer Vision**
Data Type	**Image**
Data Environment	**Supervised Learning**
Learning Paradigm	**Classification**
Explainability	**Not Explainable**

SPATIAL TEMPORAL GRAPH CONVOLUTIONAL NETWORKS

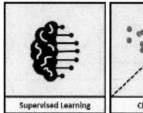
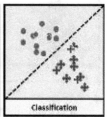

Definition	**Spatial-Temporal Graph Convolutional Networks is a convolutional neural network that automatically learns spatial and temporal patterns from data.**
Main Domain	**Computer Vision**
Data Type	**Video**
Data Environment	**Supervised Learning**
Learning Paradigm	**Classification**
Explainability	**-**

STOCHASTIC GRADIENT DESCENT

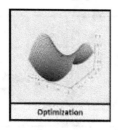

Optimization

Definition	**Stochastic gradient descent is an iterative method for optimizing an objective function with suitable smoothing properties. It can be considered as a stochastic approach to gradient descent optimization. It involves replacing the actual gradient (computed from the entire data set) with an estimate (calculated from a randomly selected subset of the data).**
Main Domain	**Classic Data Science**
Data Type	**Structured data**
Data Environment	-
Learning Paradigm	**Optimization**
Explainability	-

49

SUPPORT VECTOR MACHINE

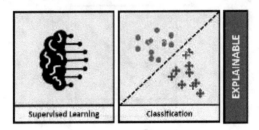

Definition	**SVM are linear classifiers based on the principle of margin maximization. They perform the classification task by constructing the hyperplane in a higher-dimensional space that optimally separates the data into two categories.**
Main Domain	**Classic Data Science**
Data Type	**Structured data**
Data Environment	**Supervised Learning**
Learning Paradigm	**Classification**
Explainability	**Explainable**

WAVENET

Unsupervised Learning

Definition	Wavenet is a deep neural network for generating raw audio waveforms. The model is fully probabilistic and autoregressive, where the predictive distribution for each audio sample depends on all previous ones.
Main Domain	NLP & Speech Processing
Data Type	Time Series
Data Environment	Unsupervised Learning
Learning Paradigm	NLP Task
Explainability	-

XGBOOST

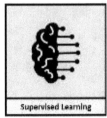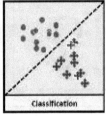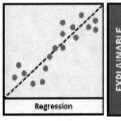

Supervised Learning	**Classification**	**Regression**

Definition	**XGBoost is an extension of gradient boosted decision trees (GBM) and is specifically designed to improve speed and performance by using regularization methods to combat overfitting.**
Main Domain	**Classic Data Science**
Data Type	**Structured data**
Data Environment	**Supervised Learning**
Learning Paradigm	**Classification, Regression**
Explainability	**Explainable**

GLOSSARY

A/B testing

A statistical way of comparing two (or more) techniques—the "A" and the "B"—typically an incumbent against a new rival. A/B testing aims to determine not only which technique performs better but also to understand whether the difference is statistically significant. A/B testing usually considers only two techniques using one measurement, but it can be applied to any finite number of techniques and measurements.

Accuracy

The fraction of predictions that a classification model got right. In multi-class classification, accuracy is defined as follows:

$$\text{Accuracy} = \frac{\text{Correct Predictions}}{\text{Total Number Of Examples}}$$

In binary classification, accuracy has the following definition:

$$\text{Accuracy} = \frac{\text{True Positives} + \text{True Negatives}}{\text{Total Number Of Examples}}$$

See true positive and true negative. Contrast accuracy with precision and recall.

Activation Function

A function (for example, ReLU or sigmoid) that takes in the weighted sum of all of the inputs from the previous layer and then generates and passes an output value (typically nonlinear) to the next layer.

Backpropagation

The primary algorithm for performing gradient descent on neural networks. First, the output values of each node are calculated (and cached) in a forward pass. Then, the partial derivative of the error with respect to each parameter is calculated in a backward pass through the graph.

Binary Classification

A type of classification task that outputs one of two mutually exclusive classes. For example, a machine learning model that evaluates email messages and outputs either "spam" or "not spam" is a binary classifier.

Contrast with multi-class classification.

Data Augmentation

Artificially boosting the range and number of training examples by transforming existing examples to create additional examples. For example, suppose images are one of your features, but your dataset doesn't contain enough image examples for the model to learn useful associations. Ideally, you'd add enough labeled images to your dataset to enable your model to train properly. If that's not possible, data augmentation can rotate, stretch, and reflect each image to produce many variants of the original picture, possibly yielding enough labeled data to enable excellent training.

Decoder

In general, any ML system that converts from a processed, dense, or internal representation to a more raw, sparse, or external representation.

Decoders are often a component of a larger model, where they are frequently paired with an encoder.

In sequence-to-sequence tasks, a decoder starts with the internal state generated by the encoder to predict the next sequence.

Refer to Transformer for the definition of a decoder within the Transformer architecture.

Dimensions

Overloaded term having any of the following definitions:

- The number of levels of coordinates in a Tensor. For example:
    - A scalar has zero dimensions; for example, ["Hello"].
    - A vector has one dimension; for example, [3, 5, 7, 11].

- A matrix has two dimensions; for example, [[2, 4, 18], [5, 7, 14]].

You can uniquely specify a particular cell in a one-dimensional vector with one coordinate; you need two coordinates to uniquely specify a particular cell in a two-dimensional matrix.

- The number of entries in a feature vector.
- The number of elements in an embedding layer.

Discriminator

A system that determines whether examples are real or fake.

Alternatively, the subsystem within a generative adversarial network that determines whether the examples created by the generator are real or fake.

Embeddings

A categorical feature represented as a continuous-valued feature. Typically, an embedding is a translation of a high-dimensional vector into a low-dimensional space. For example, you can represent the words in an English sentence in either of the following two ways:

- As a million-element (high-dimensional) sparse vector in which all elements are integers. Each cell in the vector represents a separate English word; the value in a cell represents the number of times that word appears in a sentence. Since a single English sentence is unlikely to contain more than 50 words, nearly every cell in the vector will contain a 0. The few cells that aren't 0 will contain a low integer (usually 1) representing the number of times that word appeared in the sentence.

- As a several-hundred-element (low-dimensional) dense vector in which each element holds a floating-point value between 0 and 1. This is an embedding.

Encoder

In general, any ML system that converts from a raw, sparse, or external representation into a more processed, denser, or more internal representation.

Encoders are often a component of a larger model, where they are frequently paired with a decoder. Some Transformers pair encoders with decoders, though other Transformers use only the encoder or only the decoder.

Some systems use the encoder's output as the input to a classification or regression network.

In sequence-to-sequence tasks, an encoder takes an input sequence and returns an internal state (a vector). Then, the decoder uses that internal state to predict the next sequence.

Refer to Transformer for the definition of an encoder in the Transformer architecture.

Epoch

A full training pass over the entire dataset such that each example has been seen once. Thus, an epoch represents N/batch size training iterations, where N is the total number of examples.

Feature Extraction

Overloaded term having either of the following definitions:

- Retrieving intermediate feature representations calculated by an unsupervised or pretrained model (for example, hidden layer values in a neural network) for use in another model as input.
- Synonym for feature engineering.

Feature Set

The group of features your machine learning model trains on. For example, postal code, property size, and property condition might comprise a simple feature set for a model that predicts housing prices.

Feedback Loop

In machine learning, a situation in which a model's predictions influence the training data for the same model or another model. For example, a model that recommends movies will influence the movies that people see, which will then influence subsequent movie recommendation models.

Few-Shot Learning

A machine learning approach, often used for object classification, designed to learn effective classifiers from only a small number of training examples.

Generalization

Refers to your model's ability to make correct predictions on new, previously unseen data as opposed to the data used to train the model.

Heuristic

A simple and quickly implemented solution to a problem. For example, "With a heuristic, we achieved 86% accuracy. When we switched to a deep neural network, accuracy went up to 98%."

Hidden Jayer

A synthetic layer in a neural network between the input layer (that is, the features) and the output layer (the prediction). Hidden layers typically contain an activation function (such as ReLU) for training. A deep neural network contains more than one hidden layer.

Hyperparameter

The "knobs" that you tweak during successive runs of training a model. For example, learning rate is a hyperparameter.

Implicit Bias

Automatically making an association or assumption based on one's mental models and memories. Implicit bias can affect the following:

- How data is collected and classified.
- How machine learning systems are designed and developed.

For example, when building a classifier to identify wedding photos, an engineer may use the presence of a white dress in a photo as a feature. However, white dresses have been customary only during certain eras and in certain cultures.

Inference

In machine learning, often refers to the process of making predictions by applying the trained model to unlabeled examples. In statistics, inference refers to the process of fitting the parameters of a distribution conditioned on some observed data.

Learning Rate

A scalar used to train a model via gradient descent. During each iteration, the gradient descent algorithm multiplies the learning rate by the gradient. The resulting product is called the gradient step.

Learning rate is a key hyperparameter.

Loss

A measure of how far a model's predictions are from its label. Or, to phrase it more pessimistically, a measure of how bad the model is. To determine this value, a model must define a loss function. For example, linear regression models typically use mean squared error for a loss function, while logistic regression models use Log Loss.

Model

The representation of what a machine learning system has learned from the training data.

Multi-Class Classification

Classification problems that distinguish among more than two classes. For example, there are approximately 128 species of maple trees, so a model that categorized maple tree species would be multi-class. Conversely, a model that divided emails into only two categories (spam and not spam) would be a binary classification model.

Pre-Trained Model

Models or model components (such as embeddings) that have been already been trained. Sometimes, you'll feed pre-trained embeddings into a neural network. Other times, your model will train the embeddings itself rather than rely on the pre-trained embeddings.

Recurrent Neural Network

A neural network that is intentionally run multiple times, where parts of each run feed into the next run. Specifically, hidden layers from the previous run provide part of the input to the same hidden layer in the next run. Recurrent neural networks are particularly useful for evaluating sequences, so that the hidden layers can learn from previous runs of the neural network on earlier parts of the sequence.

For example, the following figure shows a recurrent neural network that runs four times. Notice that the values learned in the hidden layers from the first run become part of the input to the same hidden layers in the second run. Similarly, the values learned in the hidden layer on the second run become part of the input to the same hidden layer in the third run. In this way, the recurrent neural network gradually trains and predicts the meaning of the entire sequence rather than just the meaning of individual words.

Sequence-to-Sequence Task

A task that converts an input sequence of tokens to an output sequence of tokens. For example, two popular kinds of sequence-to-sequence tasks are:

- Translators:
    - Sample input sequence: "I love you."
    - Sample output sequence: "Je t'aime."
- Question answering:

- o Sample input sequence: "Do I need my car in New York City?"
- o Sample output sequence: "No. Please keep your car at home."

Sigmoid Function

A function that maps logistic or multinomial regression output (log odds) to probabilities, returning a value between 0 and 1. The sigmoid function has the following formula:

$$y = \frac{1}{1 + e^{-\sigma}}$$

where in logistic regression problems is simply:

$$\sigma = b + w_1 x_1 + w_2 x_2 + \ldots w_n x_n$$

In other words, the sigmoid function converts into a probability between 0 and 1.

In some neural networks, the sigmoid function acts as the activation function.

SoftMax

A function that provides probabilities for each possible class in a multi-class classification model. The probabilities add up to exactly 1.0. For example, SoftMax might determine that the probability of a particular image being a dog at 0.9, a cat at 0.08, and a horse at 0.02. (Also called full SoftMax.)

Test Set

The subset of the dataset that you use to test your model after the model has gone through initial vetting by the validation set.

Time Series Analysis

A subfield of machine learning and statistics that analyzes temporal data. Many types of machine learning problems require time series analysis, including classification, clustering, forecasting, and anomaly detection. For example, you could use time series analysis to forecast the future sales of winter coats by month based on historical sales data.

Training Set

The subset of the dataset used to train a model.

Transfer Learning

Transferring information from one machine learning task to another. For example, in multi-task learning, a single model solves multiple tasks, such as a deep model that has different output nodes for different tasks. Transfer learning might involve transferring knowledge from the solution of a simpler task to a more complex one, or involve transferring knowledge from a task where there is more data to one where there is less data.

Most machine learning systems solve a single task. Transfer learning is a baby step towards artificial intelligence in which a single program can solve multiple tasks.

Transformer

A neural network architecture developed at Google that relies on self-attention mechanisms to transform a sequence of input embeddings into a sequence of output embeddings without relying on convolutions or recurrent neural networks. A Transformer can be viewed as a stack of self-attention layers.

A Transformer can include any of the following:

- an encoder
- a decoder
- both an encoder and decoder

An encoder transforms a sequence of embeddings into a new sequence of the same length. An encoder includes N identical layers, each of which contains two sub-layers. These two sub-layers are applied at each position of the input embedding sequence, transforming each element of the sequence into a new embedding. The first encoder sub-layer aggregates information from across the input sequence. The second encoder sub-layer transforms the aggregated information into an output embedding.

A decoder transforms a sequence of input embeddings into a sequence of output embeddings, possibly with a different length. A decoder also includes N identical layers with three sub-layers, two of which are similar to the encoder sub-layers. The third decoder sub-layer takes the output of the encoder and applies the self-attention mechanism to gather information from it.

True negative (TN)

An example in which the model correctly predicted the negative class. For example, the model inferred that a particular email message was not spam, and that email message really was not spam.

True positive (TP)

An example in which the model correctly predicted the positive class. For example, the model inferred that a particular email message was spam, and that email message really was spam.

True positive rate (TPR)

Synonym for recall. That is:

$$\text{True Positive Rate} = \frac{\text{True Positives}}{\text{True Positives} + \text{False Negatives}}$$

True positive rate is the y-axis in an ROC curve.

Validation

A process used, as part of training, to evaluate the quality of a machine learning model using the validation set. Because the validation set is disjoint from the training set, validation helps ensure that the model's performance generalizes beyond the training set.

Validation Set

A subset of the dataset—disjoint from the training set—used in validation.

Variable Importance

A set of scores that indicates the relative importance of each feature to the model.

For example, consider a decision tree that estimates house prices. Suppose this decision tree uses three features: size, age, and style. If a set of variable importance for the three features are calculated to be {size=5.8, age=2.5, style=4.7}, then size is more important to the decision tree than age or style.

Different variable importance metrics exist, which can inform ML experts about different aspects of models.

Weight

A coefficient for a feature in a linear model, or an edge in a deep network. The goal of training a linear model is to determine the ideal weight for each feature. If a weight is 0, then its corresponding feature does not contribute to the model.

Source:

Google, Machine Learning Glossary:
https://developers.google.com/machine-learning/glossary

[Creative Commons Attribution 4.0 License]

https://creativecommons.org/licenses/by/4.0/

Also available from the Author

THE AI THOUGHT BOOK:

Inspirational Thoughts & Quotes on Artificial Intelligence
(Including 13 colored illustrations & 3 essays for the fundamental
understanding of AI)

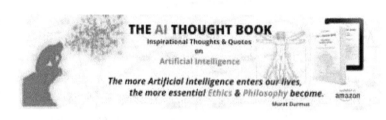

Available on Amazon:

Kindle -- Paperback -- Hardcover

An excerpt of the book can be downloaded here:
https://www.aisoma.de/the-ai-thought-book/

INSIDE ALAN TURING: QUOTES & CONTEMPLATIONS

Alan Turing is generally considered the father of computer science and artificial intelligence. He was also a theoretical biologist who developed algorithms to explain complex patterns using simple inputs and random fluctuation as a side hobby. Unfortunately, his life tragically ended in suicide in 1954, after he was chemically castrated as punishment (instead of prison) for 'criminal' gay acts.

"We can only see a short distance ahead, but we can see plenty there that needs to be done." ~ Alan Turing

Available on Amazon:

Kindle -- Paperback